SCHOOLED LIVES:
POEMS BY TWO BROTHERS

BARRY AND STEVE BENSON

BLUE LIGHT PRESS ◆ 1ST WORLD PUBLISHING

SAN FRANCISCO ◆ FAIRFIELD ◆ DELHI

SCHOOLED LIVES: POEMS BY TWO BROTHERS
Copyright ©2009 by Barry and Steve Benson

1ST WORLD PUBLISHING
106 South Court Street
Fairfield, Iowa 52556
www.1stworldpublishing.com

BLUE LIGHT PRESS
1563 45th Avenue
San Francisco, California, 94122

COVER AND BOOK DESIGN
Melanie Gendron
www.melaniegendron.com

FIRST EDITION

LCCN: 2009936901

ISBN: 978-1-4218-9135-4

DEDICATIONS

BARRY'S:

To Sally, Cory, Mark, Josef, Daniel, Sam, Kirsten.

To my dispersed writing group: Dee DePhillips, Josef Benson, Linda Stober, Sam Benson, Steve Benson.

And to those who have encouraged my writing through the years: Dr. Dwight C. Marsh, Dr. George F. Day, John Gaps III, Prof. Maureen MCoy, Dr. Rick Christman, Dr. Dale Norris, Dr. Robert F. Gish ("Writin' is fightin' so keep on fightin' ...").

STEVE'S:

For Darla, Reid, Chloe, Logan, classmates, teachers (especially Cathy Winter who made me write my first "real" poem), coaches and friends. Special thanks to our late parents, Jennie and Arnold, our uncles and aunts who let us stay with them rent-free every summer, and of course to my big brother Barry who has been there since day one.

ACKNOWLEDGEMENTS

— to the editors of the following journals, in which these poems first appeared, some in earlier versions or under different titles:

Abbey: "'Song of Solomon' Always Makes Me Sad."

The Blind Man's Rainbow: "Experience," and "Hollyhocks."

Brevities: "A Damp Drizzly Soul," "Old Man Racing Spring," and "The Tiny."

The Briar Cliff Review: "The Green Harp," "A Small Window," and "Those Nights."

ByLine: "Hidden Triolet in Brother's Pantoum Critique."

The Christian Science Monitor: "Best Country Music," "The Best Writers," "The Counter of Summer," "Ditched Bottles," "Dog Sleeping in Abstract Sunlight," "Dressy," "Experience," "Feeding Time," "From a Bluff," "From Limestone Cliffs," "Green Glory," "Morning Cargo," "An Outing on the Lake," "An Overseas Call," "Penmanship," "Spring Breeze," "Traveling Light," "Water Bearers," and "Yellow."

The Comstock Review: "Red Rover Send Someone Over."

Drumvoices Review: "Waking after the English Party."

The Dryland Fish – An Anthology of Contemporary Iowa Poets: "My Wife's Lovers," and "Sandman Dates Tooth Fairy."

FLYWAY: A Literary Review: "Sirens of Summer."

Hidden Oak: "Pieces of a Waitress," and "Po-Ling."

The Hollins Critic: "Up in the Attic."

Iconoclast: "Asian Ocean Waves and Toxin B," and "LaDonna."

Left Behind: "Candy for the Fat Lady," and "Miracle in the Men's Room."

Lyrical Iowa: "Bull Snake in the Hay Bale," "Father and Son Teaching," "Genetic Complex," "Highway 101 Night Train," "It Broke Reuben's Heart When They Burned Down the Farm," "Mulberry Art," "Private Lake Triolet," "Sexagenarian," "A Shovelful of Clay," "To Nancy, My Co-Department Head."

The MacGuffin: "The Tyranny of Memory."

MARGIE: "Mr. Blake Reports Back."

Mid-America Poetry Review: "Pulled Home," "May in Iowa," and "Staid Coffee: Always at 2:00."

The New Orphic Review: "Class Reunion," "Cryptic Words from the Tavern Man," "Prisoner of Sex — Aren't We All?"

Nibbble: "A Golden Spring," and "May."

North American Review: "Drums in Oslo," and "Rave On, Buddy Holly," "Vermeer's Nails."

Plainsongs: "Alone with the Wild Man of Borneo," "Empty Nest, Hedgehog, Canada Geese," "Friday Night Rabbit Fry," "The Last Taste," and "Strokes."

Poet Lore: "Transformation."

Poetpourri: "VAS."

Potpourri: "Fall Squirrel."

Quercus Review: "The Outdoor Life," and "Rorschach Footwear."

The Rockford Review: "Cryptic Words from the Tavern Man."

The Spoon River Poetry Review: "Mayan Magic," and "Ode to Trespass."

Subtropics: "Aunt Clara's Correspondence."

Terminus: A Magazine of the Arts: "Kick Return from Sing Sing."

Wisconsin Review: "Hollyhocks," "A Mansion by the Ocean," "My Wife's Lovers," and "Tongue in Cheek."

CONTENTS

SCHOOLED LIVES:
POEMS BY TWO BROTHERS

As You Start Your Walk

"Smell is the muse of memory and therefore the root of writing."
— Erica Jong

Apple cider in the press
or an orchard on a sunny October afternoon.
Baby skin, even the bottom, just after a bath.
Baked bread from Aunt Clara's stove.
A book — as you riff its delicious pages.

A barn's main alley and stalls at feeding time.
Burning leaves where it still isn't illegal.
Chocolate chip cookies just out of the oven.
Cut sweet alfalfa hay drying in the sun.
Flurry of leaves on your way to football or soccer.
Liniment and analgesic applied after the game.

First sense of spring in March, late February air.
Blooms of crocus, daffodil, tulips, asters, roses.
Coneflowers, pasqueflowers, azaleas, sweetpeas.
Horse flesh, leather gear tack from the stable
while you curry and comb and brush and rub.

Gas lid fumes from Harry's 50 gallon barrel.
Lake Superior in Duluth at the end of the pier
or touching the yachts aligned in Bayfield.
Clean sheets from the line and ready to fold.
Terry cloth bath towels fresh to the face
imbued with sunshine's crackly ionization.

Popcorn. Lilac bushes, pink, dark purple and
white during just two weeks in April or May.
Firewood smoke from your neighbors.
Mowed, mulched lawn grass lying in rows.
Neck hair behind the ear of your lover.

Ocean breezes from the helm, rail, or fantail
while facing the wind or gazing at your wake.
Rope sisal or hemp coiled or shouldered
or the big hawsers moored to a brace.
Winter's chill inhaled up your nose
just as you reach for a dipper of stars

(B)

HOLLYHOCKS

"The patient ardor of the unpursued."
—E. A. Robinson

Driven men first glimpse our faux bricks when
bouncing over the bushy bend in our rutted lane.
Dust from crunching wheels veils tall flocks
of hollyhocks flirting from our falling picket fence.

Shaved men miss our swaybacked barn without a flake
hiding its weathered wood. With magnetic signs
hugging doors, scented men kill motors in company
cars while sunlight ministers to black limbs

of dying elms clutching our farm's outskirts.
Men solve cement puzzles to our cracked doorstep.
A cautionary tale at rusty screens, we gaze
through eyelash gauze at hazy husband suits

declaiming company names in our selected audience.
Instead of editing men we footnote ambulatory dreams.
We're snagged in our own home when Mother casts
beyond us, hooks, reels in and lands gasping men.

Becalmed at a chrome-legged kitchen table that pulls
apart in the middle, hot strong coffee hurts lanes
down depressions in our chests. Young magicians
conjure policies stuffed into their not brief cases.

God knows we shun "pretty" with our equine face,
tangled mane, pox pricked skin and stained canines.
Our small eyes seem smudged. Our teeth are as yellow
as the out-of-tune piano keys Mother makes us pound

in the ferny parlor where our fat Bible sits on a stand.
The only men we love are in our album or in the ground.
Each dawn at cock's scream we hum a hymn to the Bald
One guiding Him to our golden mouths and hollow hands.

(S)

Two Poems Play Hide & Seek

This morning one showed me his best side
then the other teased me with a glimpse

after I clearly heard herds of words
and fancied legs and lines and feet

but not quite enough awake yet
to throw back restraining blankets

or leap from restful warmth to find
sheet of paper, pen or sharpened pencil

in still cold morning breath of work
on the chilled shiny surface of my desk

where I make respectable people
out of nothing but their business

for you to read and hear within my words
in our wakeful respectable worlds

where poems show me their sleepy faces
in my lighted clock radio's warm dial.

But now I'm up and writing at 4:07
and those two are back in hiding.

I know they'll show themselves again
tomorrow, tantalizing me. Maybe

I'll capture these two fugitives
and send my artist's sketch to you

to identify on the table of their contents
or coffee house of public performance.

(B)

THE BEST WRITERS

are spiders;
they connect everything
with fine homespun lines.
Living or dead,
it really doesn't matter.

They fish in the wind,
carefully casting silky yarns
to catch anything nourishing.
They live in the trembling
nets of their own designs.

PENMANSHIP

A longhand r
is a bird's head
with its beak lifted
as if singing or expecting
a refreshing sip of rain,
a sweet slurp of worm,
or a salty insect
to slip from the white
pantry of the sky.

(S)

SIRENS OF SUMMER

"I lean and loafe at my ease observing a spear of summer grass."
— Walt Whitman

You sense and imagine the flower, wind,
sun on grasses, through leaves and shrubs,
blue sky reflecting rounded hills,
trees, reeds, creeks, fuzzy cattails
swaying and bending in cooling breeze.

You scan a paint-bare shed once red
crib or abandoned brown-flecked barn
leaning, angling, but steadied still
by climbing clematis, morning glory vines.

Ages of men and women and children
walked and drove, bucked a tractor over
furrowed lanes, now-empty roads

until here, alone, stopping your car
this wayside calling, singing to you
sirens of summer softness
Ulysses sun, blue cool currents

enticing your tan-clothed naked body
in fleshed-out countryside all
fresh air cloud-pierced sunshine flower.

(B)

The Green Harp

Good harps make good neighbors.

Green heart-shaped notes fade,
unravel, relinquish grips
on diamond links.

I play backwards
with one gloved hand
on each side of our vibrating fence.

I tickle tangled vines
between my neighbor's yard and mine.

At fence and song's end
I hug green valentines
in my aching arms.

I carry dying hearts to the compost mound
where they slowly mix
with other plucked tunes
enriching the birthplace of music.

(S)

Alone With the Wild Man of Borneo

This July-fireball afternoon in a pasture not far from fields
where we boys baled hay in country dust and sun and sweat,

patrons stare at the geek in rags and a promise to bite
off the head of a living chicken, or it could be a snake

the barker shouts. And yes, after the geek's dance-flailing
of arms and legs, moan-muttering bicuspid-snapping,

jounce-dangled long greasy locks like dread-dipped head,
ticket-buyers pay their silver and enter the chicken-wire

roped-off section of sweating canvas top and wondering wait
in the hot enclosure for the geek to dip his unwashed hands,

draw the panic-bird up toward head-shadow close-blotted
shade-matted hair, filthy rags and frantic wings, then

bloody fury of flapping feathers and talons kicking-up dust
until those unbelievable yellow claws actually run upright

without their own head in that crisis-carnival paid-rectangle
dividing us civilians from the chosen chicken as the crowd

slowly returns to farms, homes and jobs around Colo, Iowa
as the geek and I stand together in timeout relaxing-real.

No chains, but my words: "Man, you must be hurting for a job."

(B)

CANDY FOR THE FAT LADY

She bulged in the bed
of a parked pickup truck
where it cost two quarters
to gawk at her 1000+ pounds.

While the traveling carnival
was still pitching its pointy
tents like lovely canvas tits
I slipped almost weightlessly

between the elephants pulling
ropes and sweaty men swearing
tattooed swinging hammers
through early morning mist.

Then I heard a sweet voice:
"Little boy? Can you come here?"
I saw a huge woman in a tent
of a dress waving coyly at me.

She had a very pretty face
and in one delicate hand
she spread a fan of dollars.
"Can you buy me some candy bars?"

"Okay!" I took the money,
ran to the store and returned
with Milky Ways and Snickers.
She always paid me one Snicker.

(S)

Aunt Clara's Correspondence

REUBEN AND I WENT TO AMES LAST NIGHT
TO LOOK FOR A TYPE WRITER
I HAVE ONLY BEEN TO TWO TYPING CLASSES
I AM NOT DOING TO BAD
LAST 2 WEEKS I HAVE NOT HAD A TYPE WRITER
I JUST PRACTICE WITH MY FINGERS & MY HEAD
SO I KEEP IN MIND WHERE THE KEYS ARE

I BETTER QUIT PLAYING AROUND
AND GET MY WORK DONE
I THINK I BETTER GO BACK TO MY CHICKENS
I KNOW HOW TO DO THEM
WELL ANYWAY I TRIED HA HA

THE PLUMS WERE NOT SO HOT THIS YEAR
I PUT A BUSHEL OF APPLES IN COLD STORAGE
BAKED A BOWL FULL FOR DINNER
DID A LOT OF CANNING AS USUAL
HAD A LOT OF STRAWBERRIES AND RASBERRIES
TOOK STEVE AND YOUR MOM A JAR DILL PICKLES
HE SAID BOUGHT ONES ARE NO GOOD

HAVE NOT SEEN MANY PHEASANTS YET
THEY WAIT TILL THE HUNTING SEASON CLOSES
WE HEAR THEM THO
WE HOPE NO SNOW FOR A WHILE YET
AS WE HAVE OUR CORN TO PICK
THEY HAVE BEEN PICKING AT DAVIS ALL WEEK

WE FINALLY HAVE NO SNOW TO DIG OUT TODAY
BUT FOG SO THICK WE CAN HARDLY SEE ROAD

THAT WAY YESTER DAY TOO
OUR CORN & BEANS ARE ALL IN THE BINS
CHICKENS IN THE HEN HOUSE AND LAYING FINE
BUT PRICE IS ROTTEN —
WE HALF TO BEEF ABOUT SOMETHING
WE BUTCHERED A HOG
SO WE HAVE SOME REAL GOOD HAM AND BACON

XMAS PARTY AT MY HOUSE THIS YEAR
WE HAD HAM OF COURSE
I WAS SO BUSY MIXING AND STIRRING
I DIDN'T VISIT MUCH WITH ANY ONE
TAKES A LOT OF FOOD FOR 23 PEOPLE
WHEN YOU ARE USED TO ONLY 2   HA
OH WELL IT WAS NICE ANY WAY
MAYBE YOU WILL BE WITH US NEXT YEAR

HOW TO GET THE BULGE OUT OF KNEES
IN YOUR WOOL NAVY BLUE UNIFORM?
YOU USE A DAMP CLOTH
LAY PANTS DOWN FOLD CREASE
LAY ON CLOTH AND PRESS WITH HOT IRON
BE VERY CAREFUL NOT TO SCORCH
WOOL BURNS EASY
DAMP CLOTH WILL SHRINK THE STRETCH OUT
HOW DO YOU LIKE THE NAVY?
WHEN ARE YOU COMING HOME FOR COLLEGE?

IT IS GETTING COLDER HERE NOW
WE ARE DONE WITH OUR BEANS
YOU SHOULD HAVE BEEN HEAR THAT DAY
WE HAD A MAN WITH A NEW FOUR ROW COMBINE
HE COMBINED 30 ACRES IN ONE DAY
REUBEN ALMOST WENT IN CIRCLES

TO GET THE BEANS TOO TOWN
HE HAULED ALL THE NEXT DAY
I SHOULD BE OUT DOING MY CHICKENS

MERRY CHRISTMAS THIS IS SECOND YEAR
NO LEFSE I WOULD SEND YOU SOME
BUT I DO NOT THINK IT WOULD BE FIT TO EAT
BY THE TIME IT REACHED YOUR NAVY SHIP
SO I'LL SEND YOU SOME PEANUT BRITTLE LATER
I'VE BEEN HIDING A BOX FOR YOU
SO REUBEN WILL NOT EAT IT ALL
HOW LONG DOES IT TAKE MAIL TO REACH YOU
HOW OFTEN DOES YOUR SHIP GET MAIL?

TAKE ADVANTAGE OF THE PRIVILEGE YOU HAVE
TO LEARN ANYTHING NEW YOU CAN
IT IS BETTER TO LEARN
WHILE YOU ARE STILL YOUNG
AND ONE NEVER KNOWS TO MUCH
LOVE AUNT CLARA

(B)

STROKES

(for a fresh young farmwife)

After showing us batik and masks
from Africa, where he caught you in
The Peace Corps, your ambitious spouse
showed us his egg-laying business housed
in climate-controlled silver metal Quonsets.

Two thousand hens lost their ovums
through wire screens where soft belts
caught the identical ovoids and whisked them
to joking workers gently packing them in crates,
then in trucks that growled down dusty county roads.

Escaping outside we saw henpecked hens
stumbling backwards over fine gray soil.
They looked funny at first, like some fowl
football scrimmage or pagan chicken-rugby scrum.
But a foreign film looped through their blinking eyes.

When we asked your handsome husband what was
wrong, he looked at you first, then he frowned
and said: "When chickens live too long in cages
something goes haywire. They walk backwards and die.
Like nervous breakdowns or strokes. Who knows why?"

Before heading home, my first wife picked
a kitten from your collection. She tied red
ribbon around the kitten's neck and named her
Flannel. She purred and napped on my wife's lap
during that short peaceful stretch of graded gravel.

Four months later I found Flannel face down
in her box as if she crash landed in her litter.
I fit her into a shoe box and shoveled her into our
backyard in town while my sobbing bride finger painted
with wet oatmeal on the floor of our bright modern kitchen.

(S)

KICK RETURN FROM SING SING

— homage to Debra Marquart

"Your dad was self exiled," chimed the barman
serving cool ones in Dad's small Sing Sing

hometown trapped by nouns repeated too often,
jailed by townspeople afraid of his action verbs

denying Dad's dreams — memories as Sicily
army mechanic fine-tuning gliders, polishing

his stand-up routine, naturally gifted with wit
but here only the cool ones to listen, question

Dad's fortified voice slurring perhaps a bit garish
in this one church town, population a few hundred

too few to laugh at Dad's tossed-off lines, bar-top
juke joint dance delivered against the certainty

of death and the singing women who sway while
he swings their tray as he describes a red horizon

to which he shouts, "Get this show on the road!
Kiss her! Quit this land-locked, jib-less town!"

Instead of chanting his non-commisioned story,
his buck and wing gig in barns and corncribs

while painting fresh lumber sawed and nailed,
slapping white buckets with brushes, glossing

songs, a musician's life, a poet's performance.
Instead of women on strobe-lit dance floors

it's a drunken squeeze of a son's unstarched collar
and a whispered, "Let's go get Aunt Lenore!"

Then after last call it's the red and black beast
where "nothing good happens after midnight"

and the crouching creature grumbles its vigil
in this one block main street Lord Randall town

where years later I visit Dad with my brother
and we spot Dad staggering out of his paint shed

of stored ladders, brushes, thinner — and hardly
thinking he kicks an empty paint bucket

high into the blue Iowa sky, end-over-end
and we gaze, we circle, anticipate its descent

where we stand, legs cocked, braced, reaching
to gather it in — a spinning, floating kickoff

hovering toward us on the five yard line
and we eagerly wait, arms out, fingers loose,

a stretch, catch, a block — reel, juke and dash
each of us fixing a wild eye madly down field.

(B)

FRIDAY NIGHT RABBIT FRY

(for A.G.B. 1913-1988)

Turning from the sleeve-polished bar
he flinched, slapped by the screen door.

My eyes adjusted from sober sunlight.
He stared at me forever for a moment.

Then he climbed onto the bar and waved
his jacket from the shipwreck of his marriage.

The bartender winked and talked him down.
"Show your son to a booth, Ben. I'll send some

rabbit over when it's done." Duct tape bandaged
dark cushions that sighed from mouth-like slits.

Yellowed from forty years of smoking cigarettes
his fingers were speckled from painting houses.

We watched weird forms of foam slide down
the curved insides of our shining glasses.

Someone served us scorched chunks of rabbit.
In the patched booth we chewed the tough muscles

that once jumped over purple clover in the wind.
We piled bones on our thick white platters.

(S)

CRYPTIC WORDS FROM THE TAVERN MAN

At nine inside I sensed that world of men:
stale draught beer and sounds of pool hall
pin ball, punchboards along one wall and then

pool sticks click against those colored balls
of stripes and solids under an August sky
ricocheted beaded rawhide, grey-blue walls

and fingering pinball flippers snapping I
careened steel ball bearings off polished glassed
big-breasted women flashing rouge-powdered eyes

across wood floors with sawdust around brass
missed spittoons and beer spilled midst new cheers
over glaring games declaimed as gross and crass

through shade in concentrated cones and fears
of loss at billiards, cribbage, games of the day.
In a shadowed corner a man who reeked of beers

declared at work he heard Dad reciting poetry
of Richard Lion Heart, Ulysses, Idols of Kings
and other classics from England and Norway.

Now years since Dad had memorized ancient rhymes
I begin to comprehend his message in these lines.

(B)

STIRRING TIME

Staring down into the twister
in his tall clear tumbler
my son stirs chocolate
into his white milk.
His clinking spoon
spins me to 1951.

I'm five, sitting at a cool marble-
covered counter in a corner
drugstore with propellers
stirring time under an
ornate punched tin
silver ceiling.

Rowing my chocolate milkshake in
slow circles with a silver oar
clinking on my glass boat,
I grin at my young dad
on a red & silver
seat like mine.

He's wearing his painter's cap
with the bill bent up. His
tan pants and torn T-shirt
are speckled with colors,
some dots fresh, others
are cracked and dry.

He still has several years before
Mother will divorce him for
drinking his paychecks

at the tavern where
my brother and I
coax him home.

I hold the cold flat counter
with both hands, tuck in
new sneakers and spin
myself back to here,
leaving my father
in 1951 again.

(S)

BULL SNAKE IN THE HAY BALE

BIG BULL SNAKE yet so pleasant a work of beauty
so feared and universally taught to be shunned
hanging from a bale in a sunny Iowa alfalfa field
while we thought football and baled hay and talked . . .

big bull snake's cold eye protruding so balefully
under cold diamond pattern of perfect motif scaled skin,
closest to a diamond-back rattler Steve and I'd ever seen
writhing, wriggling to free itself from strapped bale

from the mowed and raked hay of afternoon pleasures
its stiff shaped hardness held by tight dun itchy twine
we could easily loosen so softly so wildly so easily
so huffing puffing blowing this whole hay house down

I wanted to touch it to hold it to stroke it in hand
caressing head and watching forked black tongue maybe
spewing feeling for me sensing smelling feeling my touch
although of course I knew there could be red fangs biting

or white poison diamond back green water moccasin pain
so I wasn't brave that time to risk what I didn't know then —
a lesson I learned later that nothing is what you first think
or are told should be and what later comes out of a bale!

(B)

Finding a Used Book of Poetry
With Every Page Bent Along the Edge

It's fun to imagine
this book was gripped
by a weight lifter wearing glasses
rediscovering — after years
of pumping protein into his poses —
the strength of his mind
and his forgotten love
for strong writing.

Or a grandfather farmer —
who rode a bucking tractor
while keeping his rows true
with every turning of the plow —
when it rained, relaxed on a hay bale
in a barn, reading this book
through a powerful magnifying glass
that he hid from his wife between boards.

Or a strong working mother
who, with half a dozen children
found, somehow, between cleaning,
cooking, washing dishes, folding laundry,
an hour or two every week to rest and read
the poems in this book
in her carefully edited kitchen
published in the polished chrome of a toaster.

(S)

CORY'S FIRST GAME — TOLD BY HIS DAD

I approach the park with hesitant concern
that Cory might not start or play or do well

in this his first effort at doing on his own.
But how proud I am when he leads off in the first:

"Cory Benson on second," yells his coach to the team
chattering and anxious in the first-base-line cage.

Cory cocks his hat, and from under his visor,
worn low like his first cap, he studies the pitcher

then drives a foul at his team in the dugout.
After a called strike, he cracks out a hit

that lines over first. And Cory is on!
After a walk he steals third and tries home

and beating the throw he races across the plate
as his teammates explode and I can finally exhale.

As I sit on the bleachers he finds me with his eyes
and his smile flashes his dimpled satisfaction

as I signal with one hand fisted high and I smile
while Cory is hugged by the rest of his team.

He has scored the first run after getting the first hit
for the Giants this year: Cory's initiation at eight.

(B)

A Catcher Meets His Muse

The only Muse I ever met and caught was called Kenny.
Every summer at the city pool I splashed into his ken
with his freckled face, beefy body and goofy grin.
His can openers off the high board doused lifeguards
enthroned above us all on their high chairs looking down
their white noses as if they dipped them in some royal cream
of which we jealous thrashing mortals could only dream.

Kenny Muse had the best pitching arm on our baseball team.
Every summer I was his catcher of choice, toiling in the happy
dust behind my sweaty mask, chest protector, and shin guards.
His curve cut across the mystical white pentagram of home
half buried in the storied dirt of the green diamond glowing
at the center of the county fairgrounds where the creek flooded
every seventh year in a watery thoughtless natural revolution.

In a leaky rowboat Kenny and I caught carp, catfish and bullhead
sailing over that drowned diamond, paddling with bats and boards
around the horn, sailing from first to third without touching any
submerged bases. When the runaway water returned to its normal
bed, the sun cooked dead fish and cracked mud into a baroque
stink that always makes me think of Kenny Muse, the only muse
I ever knew and caught and tossed back whatever he pitched.

(S)

MAY IN IOWA

It's the lilacs,
the flashes of yellow
goldfinches
in a swinging feeder,
wild turkey
woods walkers and
mushroom hunters,
sun-soaked tree leaves,
hum of bees
over French dandelions,
clip of tulip heads,
first crop of rhubarb,
jonquils and blue iris
or purple peonies,
a windy day
for a walk
along Walnut Creek,
May Basket Day,
Norwegian Siende Mai
— but really
it's the lilacs.

(B)

GREEN GLORY

They wait: Earth's wild seeds.
"Weeds," we sneer. Quietly
green scouts crack concrete,
strangle power stations,
disrupt communications, choke
even dirt and gravel roads,
surround towns and farms —
ready to return everything
to its green glory.

DITCHED BOTTLES

Wind hums across
chipped glass lips
thrown through
scratchy hoops
of wild berries
near deer paths
that veer back
into a valley
where every May
the same apple tree
throws its white bouquet.

(S)

RAVE ON, BUDDY HOLLY

Rave on, Buddy Holly, like Dylan
raging against the dying of the light.
Rave on, Buddy Holly, you wild man
and catch the sun at the end of the day.

Rage on, Buddy Holly, for the golden friends
and for the light-footed boys —
for the brooks too broad for leaping.
Rage on, Buddy Holly, rave on.

Rage on for us who are left,
Buddy Holly, one of these days, oh yeah!
Our midnight candle sways to your music.
We hear and see your brightening glance.

We remember so early in the morning,
Buddy, getting up a game, calling our friends
to run, laugh, yell. That'll be the day,
and then it's so easy to not go gently.

So rage on, rave on, Buddy Holly,
for us who are left, rage on
and sing to us that it doesn't matter,
Buddy Holly, any more any more any more

(B)

THE BIRTHPLACE OF ART

"Buddha saw that this world of delusion was really a burning house."
— Bukkyo Dendo Kyokai

Red flames read the black braille of burning boards.

Teeth-clenching firefighters aimed braids of water
at the smoking shell of our eleventh rented home
that crashed before dawn to our father-abandoned lawn.

It was fun watching that drafty old structure fall
into shiny chunks of ancient cave-old charcoal.

It was fun sketching animals and people on sidewalks
with charred sticks salvaged from the reeking wreckage.

It was fun watching neighbors in bathrobes and slippers
speak to each other under smoke-genies, flames and stars
reflecting in their eyes and shining on their bare skin
as they watched spark-spirits fly into the night sky.

(S)

IT BROKE REUBEN'S HEART
WHEN THEY BURNED DOWN THE FARM

We remember her mulberries and the thick white cream
from cellar and separator we cranked after milking
and poured on sweet-berries or a gooseberry pie
from the orchard we picked under Aunt Clara's keen eye.

Brother Steve and I remember hot summer haymows
before Clara's meals for combiners and threshers:

we'd help her prepare huge chicken dinners
after chasing and loop-wiring those birds on the run —
chopping-block blood, Steve chased by white fowls,
their heads chopped off, but still they would run.

We'd lick Clara's stir-spoons after angelfood cakes,
krumkaka and kringla, kumla, potato cakes, lefse . . .

Then out in the summer kitchen, corncobs and coal
we'd watch baby kittens as they'd dash in and hide
until Clara brought dinner scraps which she prepared
with bread, gravy, eggs, warm from the henhouse.

"Now all of it's gone, only switchgrass remains,"
says retired Dean Larson, in charge at St. Paul's.

(B)

MULBERRY ART

I climbed into mulberry trees
while my Aunt Clara — tall, bony, busy —
in a dress stitched from feed sacks
stretched canvas over waving grasses.

Clara crawled on henpecked hands and knees
smoothing the sailcloth (speckled, I see now,
like a Pollock Painting) on a breezy
sunny hillside in the Midwest.

She waved to me through shiny leaves
and shouted: "Okay you monkey!"
Grinning, I jumped from limb to limb
while berries thumped the loose drum.

After red and purple hail fell on the rippling sail,
Aunt Clara yelled: "Okay monkey, climb down."
Then we poured the juicy jewels into zinc pails
and pulled our painting to the next fruitful tree.

(S)

STAID COFFEE

Always at 2:00

"She's from Jasper's side of the family,"
says Cousin Betty, sitting under a still life
of a farmer's woman holding a hen
and next to the only man at Cousin Lorraine's
annual Jacobson coffee in Story City.

A reading recovery teacher from Boone says,
"My husband has nothing going on right now,"
as Lorraine pours coffee from a silver pot
while the man itches to rise but determines to stay
and dip more white kringla into hot black coffee.

Cousin Lyla announces she's read novel after novel —
"Forty alone just from the Christian library
at Immanual Lutheran Church. You tell me,
with Cecil and the kids all gone, what could be worse
than long afternoon hours from 4 to 6? They're awful."

"Old Joe Sunnoc and Grampa H.O. drank together
and why the hell not, hard as they worked that farm?
No, farming's not in my blood, that's for damn sure."
The man smiles again to both Cousin Betty and
retired librarian, Phyllis Frette, who nods her assent.

"Visiting as a kid was great, but working a farm
sunup to sundown? No way. And old H. O.
worked the family as hard as he worked the farm."
He looks out onto Main Street and watches a woman
walking from a white van to deliver a flower.

(B)

THE TYRANNY OF MEMORY

When I see a woman's shadow,
black on a shade of yellow,
I remember my music teacher
who lost a breast to cancer.

Walking past her home at night
I looked up at her bedroom light.
Once I watched her like a test
getting her shadow slowly undressed.

When I hear a phone's ringer
and I pick up the receiver
and speak, but there's no answer,
I remember my lonely father.

He'd call me in junior high
and act like a fool and cry,
asking me over and over
if I was still there . . .

When I hear a lark's tune
pouring from a fence post in June
I'm a white-haired boy dreaming at noon
under milkweeds and a horn of moon.

Staying with Aunt Clara on her farm
I fed the pigs and chickens in the barn —
sleeping to the sounds of pig feeders
and waking to the screams of roosters.

When sparrows chatter
in the shadow of a grain elevator
like the giant gnomon on a sundial,
I know I'll be here for a while.

I grew up in a small town
and I'll never live it down,
a willing victim to the tyranny
of a Middle Western memory.

(S)

Genetic Complex

Mother told us it was the handsome man's inferiority complex
that led to problems from all the drinking
by our father.

So, yes, I thought that was reason for his erratic behavior
until dashingly prominent Uncle Walter "Buster,"
grain and lumber businessman

suffered a nervous breakdown after great Aunt Myrtle's
slow tumoral death and he couldn't continue
as family executor.

So it wasn't just the drinking causing family stomach pains,
ulcerogenic surgeries and seepage
over our rented floors.

And now after 30 years performing in front of classes
I'm Ralph Ellison's Invisible Man's shadow,
stomach clenching,

and I worry if athletic literate sons, smiling roguish youths
fall victim also from the curse of being
so Mr. Earthly Romance.

And I wonder too if it could be true as people used to say
while my brother and I were growing up,
"It must be in the genes."

(B)

A CLANGING CLARITY

—for my Big Brother, who was watching . . .

Over the North Pool Hall in a one-stoplight town,
desperate to reach the beachhead of our lone bathroom,

we Audie Murphied across the battlefield of the living room
where our young single pretty mother mothered a lanky soldier.

Drunks banged our doors instead of the wheezy whore's
across the hall, where that carnival-sized female

tried to whip-tame half a dozen scruffy beasts, all,
according to Mother, from different derelict dads.

One deadbeat nominee missing the ring finger on his
left hand itched to clutch us wiry Little Leaguers

when we jumped over him on the cabbage-stinking stairs.
Holding our breath we escaped into sunlight rinsing

and glazing finned cars. We raced to Howard's Barber Shop
where butch-waxed pals pitched horseshoes by the alley —

one safe place where close actually counted for something.
Metal U's struck steel stakes, just as dropped tire irons

clang-danced on oil-soaked cement in the Shell Station
across the street where every door stood invitingly open,

welcoming us into the mysteries of motors, mufflers, MAGs,
grease, oil, plugs, and calendars of curving winsome women.

(S)

April Shakes Her Rain-drenched Hair

Spring doesn't arrive until snow vanishes
from neighbors' fence-lined backyard shade.

Crocus, tulips, daffodils, shoot-sprout out
from still winter melting mounds of white.

Bluejays screech, wreak havoc near the feeder.
Rhubarb leaves corkscrew from a standing hill.

Magnolia trees blossom before they leaf.
Bluebirds race for first arrival with the lilacs.

Wildflowers light, invite metaphors: prairie
smoke, pussytoes, buttercup, dent de lions.

(B)

RED ROVER SEND SOMEONE OVER

A red crayon over rough white paper
draws circles around Mother's red lips
kissing tissues before kissing soldiers
on the rumpled sofa in the living room
in a condemned house below flood level
across the street from kindergarten
where a gold tongue licks a ticking face
while we all snore on rugs on the floor
dreaming of trolls waiting in the hall
for recess to send us screaming over
bridges where creatures catch and eat us
if we aren't brave and fast and eager
to reach the other side of our fears.

A red crayon over rough white paper
draws circles around craters of TB tests
on our small shoulders balancing bouncing
pogo sticks on scuffed dirt and cracked
cement with legs lost to cancer and Vietnam
car wrecks heart attacks liquor and drugs
red rover red rover they've pinned us down
send someone over with napalm clutching
withered weeds picked under the swing
to bring some color to the king's daughter
riding on the teeter-totter dotting
later all the i's and buzzing flies
around the rotting bodies in the paddies.

A red crayon over rough white paper
draws circles around chipped red bricks
under a fire escape where we slipped

into our secret post office under the black
iron kissing stamps on letters of pleasures
to each other's future failed marriages and kids
who always need more than we can possibly give
never noticing our shabby clothes and cowlicks
in the burning jungles on the rough stone steps
of our ugly friendly school in the light bouncing
between our focused faces kissing and kissed
by sunlight pouring balanced without asking
if we wanted to grow straight into our deaths.

(S)

Po-ling Entreaty: Best English Class

—homage to Po-Ling

This is best English class I have taken.
My English courses I took in my countries
were emphasized grammar and so
we didn't have time to speak and write.

I took two English courses at ISU,
both of the instructors are TA and so
they didn't have the good writing skill as you.
There is still something I will suggest

for the students the English is second language
such as me, the most difficult thing is diction.
How can we choose "good" words for writing?
The only way is to read a lot. International

students usually speak and write other language
in our normal lives. How can we use the "good"
words in English learning time — is the item that
you could emphasized in the future.

Mr. Chen is one of respectable people I know
in my life because he not only teach me English
but also give kind advice from his experiences
he taught me at cramming school once each week.

I respect him and I would like to speak English
like him. He tell me after work I read paperbacks
for improving my syntax. And he say to take class
in America to speak and write. I take you class.

(B)

SANDMAN DATES TOOTH FAIRY

Children still believe he slips
into their dim rooms and sprinkles
crystals over long lashes and rapid lids.

Kids debate if Sandman should date
Tooth Fairy saddled with her blue velvet
purse of ticking hollow rootless milk teeth.

These two rendezvous at a sidewalk café
before dawn, talking work while does
and frail fawns lick blue dew.

The Tooth Fairy reaches under a wet
table to pet with a pickpocket's precision
Sandman's dark leotards sewn with rhinestones.

They collate kids' dreams shuffled out of sequence
where cute cars called Cindy or Sammy, with only
fun and games under their propped bonnets, purr

in furry tunnels where fatherly firs
blindly insert their thirsty hairy roots
before dancing in circles around stalwart stones

chiseled with spirals and Vs of geese.
During daylight The Sandman works
with busy city crews repairing

streets and playground equipment where warring
kids cavort, a few missing teeth and some
a tad aggressive from lack of sleep.

Tooth Fairy punches a time clock at City Hall
tallying licenses for births, marriages,
boats, cars, divorces and deaths.

The only evidence of their relationship is this:
Tooth Fairy flicks sand from her breasts,
Sandman picks teeth from his sheets.

(S)

Return of the Otter

Snow bunting on fencerow,
eagle nest, cold front,
geese over open water.

Vaulted clouds chill
a gem-clear quiet of pine,
nature's festival of trees.

Sole crunch crush of weight
stillness from snowy tread,
paper tossed, dog's bark.

Under glimmering moon
endangered otter returns
to lark, with wild turkey.

(B)

On Your Land

so much of what you described
today of the tree-lined
northwest corner of your acreage
of the sap and dew on your hands,
spears of summer grass,
your plantings of the new trees

I would lean and loaf,
observe, listen to you
discuss while I watch
you sway and bend,
quote the poem
like Whitman, transforming

your voice from outside
here among the trees

(B)

Out of an Arkansas Night

A ruffled roadrunner
clapping wings exploded
from leafy shadows
then zipped on into darkness
as someone quipped
(we all laughed)
"Wile E. Coyote could be next"
when a fiercely focused fox
happily furry and wildly hungry
hurried right below our row
of hazardous humans
as it chased the two-legged meal
not wasting one glance
in our direction
smiling, maybe already tasting
the feathery struggling
sweet bloody meat
death throws
at its blurred feet
running over the clear scent
(its nose grazing the ground)
the roadrunner left like an easy street
with simple signs any fox could follow . . .

Speechless
we all sat there on that braced deck
feeling outfoxed.

(S)

Empty Nest, Hedgehog, Canada Geese

The empty nest I pass near 68th and University
as I walk the mile to work at school today
preparing to conference with parents of seniors
moves me past cliché this early spring morning
as we prepare for the permanence of moving on

just as that hedgehog in the vacant field I cross
at Buffalo and 72nd near Sam's Wal-Mart parking grinder
where now the new bank is rising from the ground,
where that pudgy hedgehog moved earth for me last fall
and sent startled electric shock before my step

right next to Walnut Creek where overhead
three Canada geese further taught me lessons
about moving on – honking out I'm not alone,
we're not alone and shouldn't be afraid
of natural changes and leaving empty nests

as I cross the construction site now dirt and rising bank
once primrose, bluebell, nettle and bramble berries
and I realize we all can open or close our eyes as each day
brings familiar signs of spring or fall and adds
beginnings for each and every one of us to choose.

(B)

Best Country Music

Between lines of corn
meadowlarks pour clear sweet tunes
from fencerows at noon.

Counter Of Summer

White-capped silos wait
like salt shakers on the green
counter of summer.

From a Bluff

Dangling tree pods
in the sun's hazy white webs
practice their green peace.

(S)

Morning Cargo

Along coasts at dawn
light freighters ship darkness back
to where it belongs.

An Outing On a Lake

Between motorboats
baby ducks are following
their bouncing mother.

Yellow

butterflies scribble
through a blue journal between
fluffy erasers.

(S)

Hidden Triolet
In Brother's Pantoum Critique

— from Steve

It's so hard to hear one's own particular voice
though I admire your efforts within this form
and for practicing pantoums you give good advice

but it's hard to do one well in my own voice.
You enjoy the ride inside when you make this choice
but for me the form is a roller coaster storm

of slow climbs, repeated rhymes — just not my voice
though I admire your efforts in this fixed form.

Private Lake Triolet

this living lake has a life of its own
that comforts this bicyclist to linger or stay
for interest or withdrawal on Nature's loan

this living lake has a life of its own
under breeze-lapped shore, cirrus clouds, sun sown
though the seductive rippling water weighs

gold — this living lake has a life of its own
that comforts the visitor who lingers or stays

(B)

THE TINY

yellow bird
of poetry
stays
in the
quiet
eye
of a
storm
of imagery
guarding
her one
fresh
egg
of language
framed
by
noise.

SPRING BREEZE

Patient pines
ply needles
softly enough
to sew clouds,
stitch mist,
darn gray sky
to gray coast
until the coast
is clear.

(S)

CLIPPER BUZZ

— to Linda and Dee

I become Walter Mitty every month
walking into neighborhood Clipper Buzz
for hair cut, blow dry, incidental massage,
olfaction titillation, trimmed ear fuzz.

My hair technician surely is aware
my tip doubles each time with tactile flair
she brushes breast on shoulder, back or arm,
her fingers deftly stroking through my hair.

Amidst my Mitty adventure daydream escape
I'm sometimes struck with the possibility
my stylist with her scissors, comb and razor
could slice my carotid if she guessed my fantasy:

I travel back a century or more when men
and women with means purchased pleasures
in Kusadasi stalls more ornate than Clipper Buzz
with Turkoman bath, optional sensuous measures

of aroma therapy, deep muscle rubs and
additional services fashioned in my mind —
mutual exchange concocted out in sums
determined from phantasmal literature I find . . .

hourglass cups for tea on dainty saucers,
steam bath, soft towels, crafted woven slippers
your masseuse and you both wear, and loofa
sponge of heat with English bared in whispers

permeating clouds of steamy lotion treatment
and sudsy bubbles, scented water, warming oils
on paradox marbled slabs for sensually soothing
therapeutic release from taut turmoil —

all leaving me limp when finally time to pay.
Though wonders cease, yet I am glad to say
I've learned that Clipper Buzz to me reveals
a Turkish bathhouse where my soul sense heals.

(B)

THE SHAVER

He was cutting it close to sixty.

He asked me where "exactly"
the doctor was going to cut me.

I had no idea.
"He never said I'd be shaved."

The shaver shook his bald tanned head.
With a grin playing around his lips he said,
"But if I do it wrong he will be mad, right?"

We laughed while he gently buzzed
the base of my thumb, the back of my hand
and my wrist while he talked about his
travels around the world.

"I've toured Europe twenty times and I've loved
every minute. The best trip was the trans-Siberia
railroad back when it was dirt cheap, communist
of course. Now I couldn't afford it."

"He shaved me professionally for my surgery,
wished me luck, packed his battery-powered clipper,
then he journeyed on to the next prepped patient.

(S)

"Song of Solomon" Always Makes Me Sad

she says after I pay her my $3.75 for
my place in the short term parking zone
at the Des Moines International airport

after exchanging amenities and observations —
she on progress of the hi-rise parking garage
and me about workmanship skills of laborers.

"It's interesting to watch it go up," she says.
"It's what you have to look at all day," I joke.
"Yes, but I do get to read a lot," she observes

holding her Bible. "Any other books?" I wonder.
"No, pretty much my Bible," she turns and nods.
"What're your favorite books in the Bible?" I ask.

"Psalms, Proverbs." She smiles, cocks her head.
"I like Ecclesiastes, Song of Solomon," I remark,
"books of poetry, along with Job — and yours."

"Song of Solomon always makes me sad," she says
as I begin my shift from neutral into drive,
"what with being alone." As she beams a grin

I notice gray hair, green-blue lilt to her eyes
while I wave, exit, and reflect on our lives.

(B)

Transformation

A rabbit
leaping between the headlights of my wife's fast car
on a blacktop highway
between two cornfields
grown head high
at 2 a.m.
becomes an owl.

My wife pulls over to the loose shoulder,
gets out, looks back
at the empty road.
No owl. No rabbit. Nothing
but darkness and light
applause from long
hands of corn.

Traveling Light

I'm planning a long journey.
I'm only packing everything
we did and saw and said.
It all fits inside a memory
much smaller than my head
and weighs nothing.

(S)

LaDonna

guiding me inside my empty house, others away, not expected back
soon, LaDonna shutting doors: "Your mother and mine are gone. . ."
Day before, squatting/straddling cultivated rows, shucking peas,
we eat of freshness in neighbor Karen's mother's extensive garden.

LaDonna pulling all the shades, and pillows from the couch,
LaDonna playing house, I'm looking up into LaDonna's face, listening,
seeing so intent LaDonna's smile perched this while above me — much
later reminding me of her brother Bobby's squinting eyes,

emerald forest foray, Bobby's bark-peeled birch pole, improvised
fence vaulting (trophies, ribbons later); also her older brother Gene's
laser eyes aiming his rifle at balanced tin can where my cap should be
and how I kept stats for his crazed exploits in football pads one fall.

The path our bodies, LaDonna, fashioned before the break of trees
beyond the back field of switch grass we crawl-tamped exploring.
Those years before Pearl bought LaDonna her boarding horse
which I would have ridden bare-back too, straddled close

behind her, arms toward her breasts helping with the reins.
I wonder who we really were though at 9 and 7 (at most) LaDonna
reaching words to me, playing house or doctor, LaDonna observing
as we had clematis, snowball blossoms outside the jade green door

before their regularly appointed time and season although neither of us
extolled this blooming as a first, it seemed to us so very natural.
And then LaDonna ran up to me like we had won this spin-the-bottle offer
to take to the river bank and play outside the North Park shelter.

Earlier, scouting agates following each other's passion over half the town: "Touch me. Do you like this? Again. Why does this make you laugh?" Now gathering back the veiled ruby valance, LaDonna, seeing no one noticing our move, LaDonna, preceding with your avid turquoise smile

drawing me to the couch, glancing, asking, "Is it in?"— more natural than your practiced dives or my 4th of July accordion band shell performance . . . until in mid-thought Pearl barging, screaming, demanding, "LaDonna, get your clothes on!" LaDonna, running for the bedroom leaving me

tongue-tied, alone: "We're doing nothing, only playing doctor!" To Pearl, to no avail — "Where is she?" LaDonna grasping frantic for her clothes . . . Pearl slapping her bare skin, her back and bottom, yanking LaDonna's ear, body exposed across the yard, dragging her naked to her house next door.

I watch LaDonna disappearing, first for one year, then more, wondering would others know – Karen or her gardening mom, Alice, too, watching from her window, neighbors talking across the streets, we not old enough to anticipate reunions or worry would these words become evaluation

penalties for broken commandments heavily handed down, small town, stopping our race through biology, certified diplomas slapped on us, LaDonna, my Navy yeoman metaphorical tattoo? Along the woods behind the Munsen mansion carriage house, LaDonna, sitting Indian style, our lost words touching

toes, heels, spreading palms. How many years avoiding LaDonna: elementary fountain queues, I'd slink to the other end, always one grade older, still afraid to let LaDonna see my imagined leaden shame we should have faced together. Then family moves before high school, mothers finished exchanging dresses

after leaving husbands. Now here I am telling others our story, knowing for so many years this was the first time, natural opalescent artesian waters then and now, LaDonna living in memory here. It's come to this, if anyone wants to know how much I want to tell it as it is, to apologize to LaDonna.

(B)

Tongue In Cheek

A trapped mollusk
stripped of its wordless shell.

Hermit dreamer in a dripping cave.

Baby leviathan trapped
in its own soft flesh.

Curious as a penis.

Eager to taste and test
all it touches or is touched by,
it salivates over pork chops
and vaginas, nipples and pickles.

Nervous, split, cracked,
it pokes, sucks, taps
teeth , gums and pink roof —
licking all languages.

Twister, liar, together
we will enter
tasteless earth
or thirsty tongues
of furious fire.

But not yet my limber trembling
member. There's still time
for strawberry ice cream
to melt on your pasture
of tiny rosebuds —

thawing all over your living
cobblestones of pleasure
split down the center
like a greasy gutter
guiding water.

(S)

Vas

Do I wish someone had told me these feelings
as a deserted house a dried-out nest an empty vase?
Would I have preferred jokes eunuchs sing sopano or
stale bags of hard popcorn kernels unfit for consumption?

I look over bills from Surgery Center of Iowa
See charges of $860 and wonder at real costs
insurance claim explanations of benefits / doctor's
note of initial symptom UNWANTED FERTILITY

I begin to understand why EKG W/INT proceeds from
initial evaluation HCP PAYMENT to PPO WRITE OFF
and how medication (NOROXIN) may cause side effects
and how THIS STATEMENT IS FOR AMOUNT
PAYABLE DIRECTLY BY YOU

KNOW HOW YOU REACT TO IT BEFORE YOU TAKE IT
MUST NOT GIVE THIS MEDICINE TO OTHER PEOPLE /
You NOTICE OTHER EFFECTS NOT LISTED ABOVE,
CONTACT YOUR DOCTOR / how HOME CARE INFORM-
ATION encourages scrotal support

ice bag intermittently to promote comfort do not walk
first two days an upright position can cause discomfort
NOTIFY PHYSICIAN IF YOU DEVELOP CHILLS
PERSISTENT PAIN
do I wish someone had told me these feelings do I know?

(B)

Miracle In the Men's Room

"Which is not to say that a poem is like going to the Men's Room."
— Richard Wilbur

When I press my dripping face to mute linen that droops
from mirrored machines in men's rooms in bowling
alleys, malls, body shops and gas stations,

I always look to see if my face released
a dirty copy of itself on the cloth's white scroll.

LOCAL MAN'S FACE APPEARS ON TOWEL IN MEN'S ROOM!
Though experts belittle its authenticity
like that disputed shroud in Turin,

what interests me is the possibility of one phenomenon
rocketing an unknown John or Joan into arcs of celebrity.

I see myself blundering from the Men's Room, grabbing
the first person passing and dragging him or her
in to witness this titillating transference.

Better make it a man; a woman might be confused:
"Hey Lady! Come in here quick and look at this!"

Better make it a man already in there
meditating at a urinal. Clutching his arm
I'd spin him around to see this local miracle,

probably pissing him off while he sprayed himself, the wall
and the floor — his penis drooping like a pink pickle.

He'd gawk at my mono-print on the talk show towel
as our futures fused famously forever until
money & fame trumped the fading wonder.

(S)

SEXAGENARIAN

his wife puns out on their
walk with a smile, touch, twinkle
to assuage a downshift

to appease, to quench
his chest stress premonition,
morning joint and bone

as in mourning a miss
on a goal line dive by inches
a knee down on the one

or a grab for the baton with
a lead by an elbow from teammate
brother for the final leg, or

"we can hope for 30 more"
and the dry arthritic cliché cropper
"it beats the alternative"

then his wife's chuckle
as she serves up a candled piece
of lemon-lime frosted cake

and straightens the slice
of his sexagenarian's puttering

(B)

My Wife's Lovers

They must wonder what she wants with me
besides the usual chatter, the clatter
of Christmas lights and lawn mower.

Yes, I'm jealous of my wife's lovers,
but only slightly since they also offer me
pleasures — sliding over my arms, back, thighs.

It breaks her rhythm when I touch her. "Yes, yes,"
she sweetly lies at my heavy-handed tries
while her eyelids flutter.

Her legs stiffen as her perfect toes
squash pillows while her lovers press
deeper at the center of her pleasure.

They move quickly, cunningly over her slowly
provoked body, waiting calmly to recover
what my blunt fingers fumbled.

Humbled, I slip sheepishly out of bed, clutching
my balled clothes to my goose-pimply skin,
leaving her lovers tapping private

codes on the pink keys of her breasts,
knowing the answers to her tests
before she poses questions.

I close the door quietly, remembering
to latch it carefully so our children
and pets won't pounce on her pleasure.

Dressing quickly in the hall, I look down
at my own callused hands and recall
lost hours we logged together.

My wife comes out of our bedroom later
swinging her relaxed lovers at her sides.
She glides into the kitchen. Smiles at me.

Takes a clear glass from a cupboard.
Fills it with cold trembling
liquid and swallows it all.

(S)

Kumi Na Saba (at 18)

> — one of authority, a builder of hope

I lived in a land where the day
was sweeter than night. I grew,
knew love, woke up. Sigh, gasp,
struggle. I drank from the cup
of strife in a land where life
was exactly that. Until death came
and the realization lived in a land
where life was a dream. Death
was the waking up.

I know I astound our class with
a possibility of dinosaurs in Africa
where a massive creature
known as Mokele-Mbemebe —
"one who stops the flow of rivers"
lives deep inside the Congo
at the edge of a swamp forest
by Lake Tele near the equator,
not far from my Tanzania home.

American scientists often come
to research about Dar Es Salaam,
our capital, an Indian Ocean port
where I sigh for virtues of humility,
wanting to improve my skills,
mastering five languages already
after British boarding schools
in Kenya with good teachers
from Ireland and New Zealand.

Learning from Shakespeare, Rossetti,
Shaw, Hopkins, Owen, Steinbeck —
I wear Khanga dress, rich colors, flowers
around my proud head, chest and waist,
dreaming of becoming an engineer.
My lingua franca name is Koku Shubira —
one of authority, a builder of hope.
A gush of wind now lifts my hair
and elevates my spirits — your student,
Lylian Muttakyawa

(B)

THE OUTDOOR LIFE

(Found Poem)

As leather is
a natural product,
it may show

various defects arising
from the outdoor life
of an animal.

Scars from tree branches
or wire fences,
insect bites

or wrinkles all
guarantee the genuine
nature of the leather.

In addition, the skin
of an animal is not
constant in thickness.

The back side
for example
is very thick,

whereas the stomach area
is much thinner
and more flexible.

These characteristics result in
different degrees of absorption
by the dyes, resulting in

variations across the leather.

(S)

To Nancy, My Co-department Head

My wife and I return from late summer vacation
to our principal's urgent phone message, but you
call first and I jokingly anticipate department woe:

"No, it's more personal," you say and I
reply, "No, Nancy! You're not leaving for Valley too!"
And you laugh until you pause and say

"I have cancer, Barry, in my left breast
and of course I'm left handed — and
I won't return to tittering adolescents
before I'm healed from this radical mastectomy."

Nancy, you know my baby girl's heart was beating
benign arrhythmia on the ultrasound I described to you
just last week — a symbol of our too too frail lives . . .

"Our principals will take my classes for six weeks,"
you say, but no one can entertain and teach as you
even as chemo flows through your palm alternate Fridays

right after you dismiss your classes
and my wife and I bring plants and enchiladas
and relay so many prayers and offers
to drive your children for you to their own teachers.

(B)

THE LAST TASTE

You drew yourself with no clothes
in the heart of a broken open oak.

No dress code required. No skin,
teeth, hair or even those hard

white relics bracing
your form's soft home.

Giant leaves draw you in
to the acorn's essence

where the blueprints are
for every root, branch, and scar.

You gladly slipped the neck bracc
and halo you wore your last year.

Through painkillers you asked your husband
to rainbow your remains over the Rockies.

Some of your ashes filmed his fingers,
so he licked them clean, tongued them

until you were gone — the last
taste of his lean woman.

Then he and your daughter
stumbled down Butterfly Mountain

past prisms of pines
shattering boulders,

drawn home by gravity's
hidden hands.

(S)

HOMONYM RONDEAU

    — to Megan

My mother's lover touches me, I fight.
I clutch a fright-flashed kitchen knife.
His hands, their breaths, loosed lacy stays,
these staid town mistress bedroom days
become my red-corduroyed studio site:

A near-naked archetypal rite,
an apartment door ajar at night.
Couched uniform proclaims his ways,
my mother's lover.

Cock-frame, cracked glass, my mind's ride,
my student's song, my assigned respite,
I sketch-write words to stay my rage.
Imaged lines from my right-brained phase
reflect a mirrored pulsing street stop light
over my mother's lover.

(B)

PULLED HOME

The last time I was pulled all the way home
by my ear was 1953
when Reynold Nordeen and I stayed too late
throwing sticky paper plates
in the vacant lot next to Hermansen's Hatchery.

I forgot to go home for supper, and my mother . . .

But before I get to the hard part
I want you to see
how the sky looked that day
over the shabby false fronts of stores
on Main Street, and how the bird-choked trees
inhaled and exhaled.

Reynold and I launched syrupy saucers
while a screen door slammed like gunshots,
and the water tower stood like a good giant
spreading darkness over the town like black batter
pouring from the tilting purple bowl of night.

That's when my mother steamed
around a corner, snagged
my ear and towed me home
where she made me take off my belt,
drop my jeans and grab my ankles.

Now she's old and does not know my name
or hers. She flutters through
a new Alzheimer's wing
where I bring my children
to see this mumbling gray-haired
thing that does not
know them.

(S)

THOSE NIGHTS

she quoted Gideon
and then she kissed him
as nightfall pillow-slipped
from midwest October guest-
dressed seamless cross-stitch
close pulled-back September
silken comforter touch of
naked crocheted gloaming

from harsh student-strained days
hooked for darkening tresses
of pre-morning un-shaded covers
layered vicissitude will o'wisps
in wrinkled sheets blanketing
each breast hand-stroke kissed
darning dark pulpit-appliqued
threads tint-pattern embroidered

cases comforting cool uncombed
interweaving longing fingers
silken soul-drop soothing touch
as she re-told the dream of an army
of 300 hand-dipping drinking
water as his hands drew her closer
darkling damp curls those three
long quotidian feather-down nights

(B)

WATER BEARERS

Hands cupped
under braids
of water

lift sweet pools
with palms
and tight fingers

connecting us to others
wearing first furs
in smoky caves

and to future travelers
sailing between singing
stars on waves of light.

A GOLDEN SPRING

of my daughter's
curling hair —
a crimped coil
of her DNA —
clings to
my pencil
sharpened and ready
for anything today.

(S)

Large Truths Delivered:

akitimiza miaka kumi na nane

she asks, waits for him to write
this day on her 19th birthday
about their walk, their wonder

as she stands so sleek, dark,
her smile, succinct, saying yes
after long conversation

transporting Tanzania, Kenya
to gaze and touch khanga, ebony
statues, dark crèches below

carefully spoken noun, verb, name
in dream film, setting everyone at ease,
no longer questioned, awkward

& what emerges, effacingly,
this interconnection of continents,
saying, "My father in America,

inside we're all just nine,"
enfolding, relaxing, articulating
shoulders, palms, arms, elbows,

knees, and her course black hair
while akitimiza miaka kumi na nane
is changing, holding them forever.

(B)

A Shovelful of Clay

—for Paul Thomas David Hirdman

God must have a weird
sense of humor. I was running
with the wrong crowd, swearing,
drinking and sleeping around.

I was digging a ditch one day
in Story City, that Norwegian
bastion, when our minister
looked down on my sweaty struggle
and offered me the annual
church scholarship to college
on the spot. I threw a shovelful
of clay over my shoulder
and said, "Sure. Why not?"

That's how I became a minister,
a part-time college counselor
and a father of three.

If it hadn't been for that lucky
shovelful of clay, there's no telling
what ditches of earthly sin
I'd be digging in today.

(S)

FALL SQUIRREL

sometimes yes even a squirrel
loses its precarious balance its
carefully composed concentration
no longer hearing the hum inside
no longer agile as always

within its own power and grace
as observers feel and express shock
first at hearing leaves and branches
from stately elms, maples, oaks
unnaturally slapped aside

then their too nonchalant notice
hurtling through invisible chutes
on a startling air slide to ground
by this falling squirrel
    at first not the action

but the thought of this action
so uncoordinated, unbalanced
accelerating as momentum
speeds one squirrel panic

feeling finally far out of its element
on its back flailing down on its luck
falling from confident preeminence
from a lofty position others see
seemingly lissomely maintained

until yes all are surprised suspended
so shocked at this sudden failing
acrobat in breathtaking flight
as a climax tethered
by invisible forces

to earth falling
finally yes
comes the
sickening
ground
thud.

(B)

Jon Olson Would Have Caught It

Today, on national TV, watching another
All-American, all-pro, NFL receiver drop
another perfect pass in his opponent's
commercialized end zone, I remembered
Jon Olson, the best pass receiver
my brother and I have ever known.

You won't recognize his name or face
unless you grew up with us in Story City.
He loved the ball into his welcoming hands.

We launched scarred spirals through shadows
while lavender daylight went deep
into teams of stars.

We launched wobbling ducks through cones
of street lamps glowing like incubators
on corners where wiry kids — thin, common,
flexible — fought free from cracked shells
of loneliness and emptiness, stumbling wet
and curious, pecking at everything edible.

Jon and my brother practiced long perfect
spirals into the future after planning
where each reception would occur: the dying
elm on the corner, the dark parked car
tilting on one flat tire, the alley's
weedy mouth with whiffs from trashcans
like head-clearing smelling salts . . .

If Jon touched it he caught it. Simple as that.
No cameras flashed or crowds roared at his poise,
size, speed, his natural coordination,
his big soft confident hands handling the ball
with perfect timing and absolute acceptance.

Just three unknown boys experiencing the joys
of throwing and catching a football
among small town shadows.

(S)

Ode to Trespass

Breeze on my face and arms, I coast the first mile from Forest
down 66th and University then onto the Greenbelt Trail
under the 73rd St. bridge along Walnut Creek and a blue shock
of coneflowers, a brilliant bush of large black-eyed Susans

toward a slight upgrade across the tracks just behind
Fiesta Mexicana (closed by the sheriff) — sense of mesquite
and tequila in the air — until an indigo bunting leads me
and later a goldfinch as I glance for poised egret or heron

and pedal no-hands toward the 5-mile benchmark totem,
fingers on thighs, back straight, angled arms pumping too
while I wonder if today I'll see a marmot waddling or mud
turtle along the trail, beaver, and if the season's right

fly with geese on wing, spot a doe with fawn, buck in rut,
velvet-antlered, or a herd of seven in Greenbelt Forest . . .
when with leaf crunch under tire I stop to stare eye-to-eye
until Jim Carty rings his bell cycling to a Y class over lunch:

Jim's spotted a red fox, bobcat (perhaps), wild turkey —
singular times where River Trail and Lake Shore Drive
turnoffs precede my usual turnaround at "Private Lake"
where "Trespassers Will Be Prosecuted."

(B)

MAYAN	MAGIC
Two clay death-heads	Two clay death-heads
grinning side by side	grinning side by side
hang from a plain nail	hang from a hammered nail
casting a lone shadow	over a square glass vase
over the white frame	containing colored rocks
of an eastern window	water and a green coil
where morning sunlight	lifting its many living
crosses 93 million cold	arms dancing with a flat
miles in 500 seconds to	spoon-faced energy that
slip through old glass	grows into all the air
(once beach sand still	allowed to mix there
missing ocean's kiss)	with elements and rare
hit by leaves flying	systems of science
past a pine shaking	building a jade form
green hairbrush limbs	with pale pubic roots
in music made by wind	curling to the bottom
before a limestone barn	of those wet pebbles
crumbling across a road	to drink and thrive
with the shape of a black	on the wide wood ledge
cat sitting as a hole in	of this antique window
its burnt sienna door	rippling like a door
and so much more!	and so much more!

(S)

NEHEMIAH PORTRAIT

After I gather your 17 photos
you've mailed over the years
I've picked my favorites
from our 40-year past to share:

your light and shadow-framed
pose in Tahitian Trader Vic chair,
for Nehemiah back-cover portrait
eliciting praise for the actual intent
of that artist photographer
(whew, isn't this a mouthful).

The statuesque grace of your family
fronting a 12-window bungalow porch
leaves me questioning my blindness
as your football Norskie prep.

"EAI" academic-music sorority pose,
wearing a slip and a lettered-pledge sign.
I'm totally obsessed with the fringe,
your poetic, creative movement and art.

White-gloved with roommates in pumps,
full-bodice, mulberry, raised-hem dress
would have so ravished my mind as I
earned my G.I. bill in the South China Sea.

Then the formal family graduation candid —
Dad with bow tie, Mom in her pearls,
your sleeveless, pink-horizontal-striped top
forming fantasies of me as photographer
so "very welcomed" into your household.

And at our reunion we contemplate choices,
your regional Coventry leadership roles,
preaching, pastoral writing, our teaching
— and that other life we might have lived.

(B)

FALLING IN LOVE ON I-35 WITH THE SUN-MAID GIRL

It's all about freshness.

Hydroplaning at 70 in a semi's taillights
reddening my rippling view, I tap my brake
and punch the cruise to a snail's 62
to better focus on the first mouthful
of potassium-rich grape cadavers cut
from coiled vines good for basket weaving.

California seedless raisins are the only ingredients.

Rotating the full red cylinder we suddenly spark.
She pictures my hungry longing. Smiling vaguely
to her left, she's dreaming of someone like me
driving alone through rain thinking of her . . .
I love how her blue eyes look away from the viewer's, not
at them like Leonardo's sinister Lisa with her sfumato smirk.

No, the Sun-Maid girl is all sweetness and sunlight.

I'd love to date her, taste her, work the vineyards with her.

She wants only what's good for me, for us. A floppy red bonnet
frames her peachy face. Loose bows dangle between her demure
breasts covered by a clean white cotton top with two blue
stripes on each short sleeve. She's so pretty her teeth look
witty. You could almost make furniture from her mahogany hair.

Sunlight centers her in a circle of white triangles . . .

Days later, safely home, the storm over, studying raisins
in my Wheaties, they resemble dried brains or purple morels,
tiny oysters, or even shriveled scrotums hinting of musk.
I'm not shocked when I check "musk" in my duct-taped
Webster's — its Sanskrit derivation lists the testicles
of a mouse! My raisin fixation fades, skids into doughnuts.

(S)

A Damp Drizzly Soul

an overcast chill mist rising
from a river oxbow under nature's
lull of a dormant restitution of hope
amidst mounting mourning winds'

leaves rustling in cyclone gusts
around sparrows in shrubs, grasses,
pine-matted ground wet from fog,
dew, sky of near-naked stark branches

then distant crows' boisterous caw
cacophonous winged alert as an analysis
of election returns flits in stiff NW wind
under blue-gray sky and sandhill crane

or eagle weaving over brown field
roadside trail and solitary interloper
wondering through wet-heavy walnut,
white oak, elm, ash, chestnut, maple

(B)

HARBINGER

color-plashed kites race
meadow larks call farmers
goldfinches brighten feeders
crocus, tulips, magnolia, iris
stake their territories
eagles toil their return
a standing blue heron
mimics a bluebird box
in a stand of daffodil and
swallows riding the winds

(B)

An Overseas Call

A field here is a field there.
A rose there is a rose here.
A stone here is a stone there.

Then why do the words "England"
and "Stonehenge" make me need
to grab my passport and fly?

From Limestone Cliffs

Tribes of white birch arch
towards Canada at twilight
twirling crisp earrings.

Unemployed clouds march
above the flipside hearings
of the sun's golden textures.

Around scorched fire rings
birch peel ancient parchment
where the black text blurs.

(S)

DRESSY

Hills leave their clay feet
in the lake all year. Winter
brings their glass slippers.

FREE WITH EVERY PURCHASE

Overnight, hoarfrost
furnished even common weeds
beauty at no cost.

(S)

Navy Vet of Adak

studying the sky
from perspective on the day
an early evening

feeling a moist chill
40 degree Mt. Moffett
Bering Sea mist float

smoke patch hiding
in williwaw wind devils
forms one Emperor Goose

sea shadow below
jade blue oceanic waves
frolicking walrus

along coastline grass
Japanese glass balls buoyant
colors in fishnets

standing on the bridge
inhale Andreanof air
warm in your peacoat

(B)

UP IN THE ATTIC

I'm talking to myself at my desk again.
School's out. Kids have raced or dawdled home
to play with their dogs or to eat chips and watch TV.
I stay on, fulfilling the requirements of my contract.

Expelled from lungs my voice escapes my mouth after
passing throat, tongue, gums, teeth and lips, leaving
this vent in my form to join humid air stirred
around the room by a tired ceiling fan.

I watch the dusty vanes turning slowly, steadily
as if a small plane crashed through the roof
of our elementary building and only the propeller
made it through into my quiet room.

I sit at my neatly organized desk and try to see
the dead pilot up in the stuffy attic surrounded
by insulation, broken desks and flat basketballs.
The jaunty tail of the trim plane protrudes from

the damaged roof below which I am neither victim
nor witness to this tragic accident. I sit here
watching the blades turning slowly, steadily,
wondering if the pilot was my age when he ditched.

(S)

Poetry Teacher Writes to Frances L. Brown, Poet on Mount Carmel Drive in Waterloo, Iowa

Let me tell my students about B. B. King,
a shiny-eyed boy hanging around your daddy
and "twisting his mouth and jerking his head
to low-down Blues" your daddy sang in Mississippi.

Let me tell them about Frances L. Brown,
cosmetologist who owned her business for 30 years,
who wrote her first poem and was hooked for life
at 47, whose father sang the Blues to B. B. King.

How I too, just as easily as you, much more easily
would mistake Virginia Creeper for Creeping Charlie
in the rural north central hills of Mississippi
known as the delta — that ground cover, not a climber

that you refer to in your poem, "Werning Woods"
as that tough vine that creeps up those trunks
and out on branches and other enchanted places
poetry takes us where we can grow by holding on.

You still see yourself "dashing down the path
through those woods feeling the sting" of your
dusty flat feet slapping the backs of your thighs
as you run. Now you run your own extended

metaphor marathon (not even slowed by
any arthritic condition, even after those 30 years
as a cosmetologist), running your own way today
with your manuscripts finding your winning voice.

And now neither of us can be "fooled by those jerky
little smiles that die before they reach the eye"
as you speak of our anger, that both of us might need
to "prime our vocal chords on the corner of a scream."

(B)

Mr. Blake Reports Back

At nine Billy Blake
saw angels in a tree.
His father wanted to whip him
but his mother saved him.

He didn't say how long the angels stayed.

At thirty Bill Blake
saw the spirit of his dead brother
rise through the ceiling
"clapping its hands for joy."

He didn't say if he was afraid.

At seventy William Blake said:
"I have been very near the Gates of Death
& have returned very weak . . . but not in
The Imagination which Liveth for Ever."

He didn't say how strong the gates were made.

(S)

ASIAN OCEAN WAVES AND TOXIN B

Josef travels from sea to see from homeport San Diego,
Chulavista, Ventura, to Big Sur Henry Miller Library,
San Francisco, San Clemente, Seattle . . .

Josef reads Conrad, Ginsberg, Burroughs, Kerouac,
Rimbaud—poet of soul, vessel to Overman Supreme
Nietzsche, Baudelaire, Dostoyevsky, Tennyson . . .

Josef's enthralled with Wolfe, Whitman, Coleridge,
the literary life of Dante, Hardy, Oscar Wilde's
rawness of Pacific seas and Asian ocean waves . . .

from weather deck of 28-day WESTPAC Navy cruise
to Pearl, Sasebo, Pusan, Philippines, Yokusuka, Tokyo,
Hong Kong, Thailand, Singapore, Saigon, Da Nang

changing en puerto scenes of mystic sunrise from
03 flight deck of USS KITTY HAWK (CVA 63) to
6 decks down F-14 fighter cargs ammo locker billet

unlike Dad's flat-bottomed 1960s LST 1073 to Adak,
or Grandad's AAC/WWII Sicily glider mechanic duty
— as another generation steams Asian ocean waves . . .

Josef finds years later the Department of Defense
"sprayed nerve and bio agents on ships and sailors
to test Navy vulnerability to toxic warfare . . ."

in the Pacific Ocean from 1964-1968 in order to gauge
how quickly poisons could be detected, how rapidly
they would disperse with decontaminate procedure

Project SHAD (Project Shipboard Hazard And Defense),
"testing effectiveness of protective gear against
Sarin, VX nerve gas, staphylococcal enterotoxin B."

Josef learns V.A. reveals "sailors could be eligible"
for health care benefits through Veterans Affairs
which "is committed to every veteran who took part,"

according to Anthony Principi, Pentagon Department's
Secretary of Veterans Affairs, who vows "to ensure
these veterans will receive the benefits they deserve."

(B)

Rorschach Footwear

A tease of tar marks the toe
of my reading wife's sneaker.
I stare at the black void until
a peripatetic peddler plants
his left foot while striding hard
with his raised right. Over a patched
shoulder his best eye blinks views
he banks in vernacular vaults — walkabout
currency minted by memories,
like wormy Granny Smiths from delicious tarts
who would rather ride brooms than sweep dirt,
or like bridgework that burns
dropping blazing political planks
into The River Of Tax Returns.

A bulging sack on the peddler's back
strums with claw hammers, books
fluttering like headless fryers,
trinkets from the lower forty-eight,
knives now banned from unfriendly skies,
plus pots and pans like the ones Henry Moore
melted lead in until his wife tossed them
and him out of her cleanly sculpted kitchen.

The peddler's best-sellers and best-smellers
are scented cakes of something new
he creates and calls "soap" which he eagerly
demonstrates by lathering his hands in creeks,
then trades with tricky females thriving
wisely beyond good roads with crossed
twigs in their teased beehive hairdos
and cloaks stitched with cats' guts.

My wife crushes a newspaper's inky wings.
She pitches me a kiss across the room
as she glides through a doorway
with the peddler riding
her rhythmic shoe.

(S)

ALLUSIONS ABOUND — (SCORE 10)?

To begin my life with the beginning of my life,
I am an American, Chicago-born — Chicago.
You don't know me . . . but that ain't no matter
about all that David Copperfield kind of crap.
In my younger and more vulnerable years
I sit in my head in a house of my imagination,
old, a scholar's house — Mistah Kurtz, he dead.

Jake says you are likely to get diseases from
foreigners. And the only thing very noticeable
about Nebraska is that it is still, all day long,
Nebraska. I sit amid my Bokonon Karass as
Mr. Dirden whispers in our ear: "The horror!
The horror!" Marlow ceases and sits apart
in the morning pose of a meditating Buddha.

He says, "Call me Ishmael," and hides a carved
bar of soap and tells me I will fall into a nervous
love with Winston. Uncle Ike McCaslin, nearer
to 80, sits with volumes of books to his right,
pages of poems to his left, and before him is an
empty canvas while "Moonlight Sonata" breaks
the silence. And he says it was the best of times.

The boys from the island hand me the conch
but don't want to speak, only to watch and listen.
Here are two mutes and they are always together
and another old man who fishes alone in the gulf.
Boo watches the argument from the corner as
The Savage and Mustapha talk of life and love
and poverty and poetry and the dog named Buck.

(B)

A Mansion By the Ocean

Swallowing a tilting wafer of dust
floating in a glass of water aging on
my baffled waterbed's hippie headboard
I'm still as much in as out of a dry dream
of signing my name Dr. Sandy Dune or Rev. Randy
Rune on a bogus medical application in the Caribbean.

Knowing my insurance plan can't cover even
a clean politician in a red Phillip Morris
suit shouting like a boy-sized bellhop
carrying bags under his eyes at a cancer
institute I doze on the fourteenth floor
of a lavish mansion over turquoise water.

In there somewhere I overhear an older
woman with a younger man in the next
room cackling at my inability to love
anybody completely. A quack needles
me with a sympathy booster while I
ponder what sleeping slice of me

submits these goofy dream scripts.
Who builds the sets, gels the lights
and tacks the tacky scrims? I wonder
if the older laughing woman is my mother
addled by Alzheimer's, or a teacher
I've gummed together from spare parts?

I'm curious why this high-rise
wets itself wading in the bulging
breathing ocean. Through open
windows widow-making combers
pounce on and suck supple sands
reflecting rippling human glands.

Just before waking I'm walking with my talking
cousin's starfish hand inking my squid fingers'
stained seascape scrimshaw sketches in our skins.
Watching a bearded man dressed in blue legends
we cross a precarious pier with seaweed socks
and dirty foam lace cuffing its rotting shins.

(S)

Whitecaps & White Hats

This day the gray sea rolls under all of us.
Our mess deck food trays slide off tables.
Boiler needs repairs, ship's without heat.
Cold invades our quarters, wrapped in diesel
engine fumes with roars and clicks
of ballast tanks, and the OUTAGAMIE lists
from side to side riding these heavy rolls . . .

Dizziness, nausea, bewilderment send sailors
to sickbay railings, tired eyes swimming in mist
of close-up whitecaps, swells and salty sprays,
seas rising, falling, waves mounting, disappearing,
ship's deck riding low in a cavern of cloned crests
crashing heavy and abrupt in the chill and tinkle
of India bell chimes arousing the officer quarters . . .

Climbing steep ladders through narrow passage-
ways by metal rooms of whirring repair machines,
dials, welded plates, steaming hissing pipes,
glowing bulbs, high humidity vapors, sailors
prodded and barked from shallow bunk-racks,
withstand cold wind negotiating narrow scuttles,
sleepy, ready at reveille for 85 enlisted white hats . . .

(B)

DRUMS IN OSLO

The sounds of crystal
breaking in the night.

A laughing woman's scream.
A young man shouting,

trying too hard to be
older, stronger, brave —

expelling his courage
on the street,

erupting from too much beer
and boasting.

Silence. Then
drums all night.

EXPERIENCE

I feel the wisdom
of a splinter in my skin
working its way in.

(S)

Highway 101 Night Train

lights off San Diego shore
reflect columns crashing
surf-timed train repetitions
 projections over-clacking

windowpane saffron imaged
Ly or Minh through a glow
of expectation toward Saigon
en tren noche-marea paralelo

coastline shadow breakers
as sailor wayfarer troupes
intent in mirrored passageway
over Nha Trang ocean waves

on luminous silk foam mist
as salty Pacific surging swells
reach far toward tawny titian
dermal smell/feel/taste Asian

ponder of tide cowled indigo
night white phosphorescent
senses, clicking wheels steal
toward Dinh Ly, Phan Minh

(B)

Waking After the English Party

Polished authors twist in windows
like branching antlers of carved wood.

Last icy castles collapse and crash
in plastic cups sticky with whiskey.

Voices of sixty thirsty talkers
vanish into the silence of 6,000 books.

Tiptoeing through the reeking rubble
a cat creeps out of her closet.

Pieces of the house rest in the wet grass
where birds publish another morning's warnings.

Leaves, twigs, torn papers, bottle caps, squashed butts
pepper frayed rugs, warped linoleum and scuffed boards.

In the bowl of the hot tub under bombing walnuts
the human broth has lost most of its sweaty flavors.

The slapped and flattered walls prepare themselves
to stand firm with new sins driven into them.

Stained ceilings still jointed at their hips
agree again to keep their distance from floors.

Amid the disaster of dirty dishes in the kitchen
an ancient refrigerator bravely shakes and grumbles.

The stark stove suddenly looks at me accusingly,
its burners blotched with the sickness of chili.

One common fly still finds the energy
to navigate a mountain range of liquor bottles.

He circles the rumpled airport of my shirt,
lands on the hairy runway of my wrist,

rubs his legs over the helmet of his head,
then looks around for something dead.

(S)

TAPS AND REVEILLE

LST ship's office yeoman
during a 4-month deployment
completed in the North Pacific

as stacks of papers slide/slither,
files topple/scatter, cabinets
bang/bend, chairs slam

into bulkheads, dent the deck
as ship sways toward Del Mar,
homeport in San Diego drydock:

blast, chip, hammer, sand, weld,
torch, scrape, paint — yells echo,
rip-rap boat pier rippling currents

reflect lapping bluegreen waters
toward Coronado, North Island,
Point Loma, red sails, gold sunset.

Reveille as another ship steams
big into port rippling waters
reflecting two new welders

working on the keel while on
either side of me along wharfs
fishing boats and piers transport

my short-timer chain of dreams
of getting out this summer to become
a book-voyaging college boy.

(B & S)

DOG SLEEPING IN ABSTRACT SUNLIGHT

Our basset hound's camouflaged fur
resembles Robert Motherwell's
"Elegy to the Spanish Republic."

Big black ovals bloom between
gray and brown blurs with one well-
licked scar on her white shoulder.

She dozes in slices of the sun,
dragging her weight across the floor,
tracking warmth this freezing afternoon.

Her long ears lift toward a freight train
passing two blocks away telling the same
old clacking jokes to laughing tracks.

FEEDING TIME

Open the dim
cramped cell
where the poem
is pacing still wild
after all the dull days
of paralyzing ease.

In fluid measured movements
each caged word
actively waits
for you to feed it
raw moments
of your heart.

(S)

Is This Poetry?

While the two former classmates reminisce
over glasses of Lambrusco he listens to her extol
the unique architecture and decor of downtown Memphis,
especially "our Hotel, the Peabody — Yes! Where those ducks
continue their march to and from the spouting fountain
in the Grand Lobby, here daily at 11:00 a.m. and 5:00 p.m."

When the ducks have retraced their waddling webbed steps
she turns, takes out and shows to him what she's been waiting
to share . . . And she asks, "Is this poetry?" —

FROM: DANIEL R. EMANUEL / EMANUEL METALS
TO: HEAD SUPERVISOR / AT&T / 1 800 555 5050 FAX

DEAR HEAD SUPERVISOR
PLEASE REFERANCE ORDER 1073407
WE ARE VERY PISSED OFF CUSTOMER
WE PLACED ORDER ON 1-23-99
WE WERE TOLD IT WOULD BE DELIVERED 1-24-99
WE CALLED 1-25-99 AND DARLENE SAID SHE WILL CHECK
AND CALL BACK — WE NEVER HEARD FROM HER
WE CALLED AGAIN AND TALKED TO AL WHO SAID HE
        WILL CHECK
AND CALL BACK — WE NEVER HEARD FROM HIM
WE CALLED AGAIN ON FRIDAY AND TALKED TO NELLIE
AGAIN SAME THING
I KNOW YOUR A PRETTY BUSY GUY BUT TOMMARROW
        WILL BE 2 WEEKS
AND WE HAVE BEEN BILLED AND STILL NOT RECIEVED
        OUR ORDER
WHAT GOOD IS LOWER PRICING IF YOU CANNOT GET
        DELIVERY

MAYBE YOU CAN LIGHT A FIRE UNDER THERE ASS AND
        GET OUR ORDER
OR SOME ONE TO CALL US BACK TO TELL US WHEN/IF
        WE WILL RECIEVE
IF NOT WE WILL NEVER USE AT&T AGAIN
AND PLEASE TAKE OUR COMPANY OFF YOUR MAILING LIST
WE SPEND ABOUT 25000$ A YEAR ON ARE COMBINED
        COMPANIES
WE WILL BE GIVING THAT BUSINESS BACK TO IBM
IF I HAD THE FAX NUMBER TO YOUR PRESIDENT
HE WOULD BE GETTING A COPY
DRE

"Obviously," she says, "our company gave bad service. But is this poetry?"

(B)

PIECES OF A WAITRESS

 —for D.M.

Each week work wears more of her life away.
Her knees are hinges where upper and lower
legs meet to stand the pressure. The pressure
each night, after food tips tables drinks
and drunks drives her home to sleep
with a man in thin dreams.

Only dimly she remembers waddling over
her father's lumpy lawn while turning slowly
into a swan. She tinkered with broken toys
in torn weeds and trampled dirt around a silver
propane tank squatting in the yard like a bomb.
It took her years to forgive his mirrors.

Under her window's moonstruck silence
a black widow, stepping out for the night
in furs, bumps into a jumpy cricket
in black jacket and spurs. They halt,
grasp each other's secret missions, then
race away in opposite directions.

Snowing salt over charred meat,
she watches perfect crystals blur
into hunger's brown landscapes.
She stabs death with a wild silver foot,
lifts it to her teeth, chews, tastes salt
telling its ancient story of madness, decay, revolt.

She tears an apple from a tree, twists
the stem, breaks the speckled skin, sucks
juicy flesh, rips open the dry pocket
of seeds within, chews, swallows, grins.
Heavy with beauty, beams of sunlight
crash across the bones of her hands and feet.

(S)

FATHER AND SON TEACHING

My son Joe received
The Collected Works of Emerson
for Christmas this year
from his girlfriend Sarah.

They start college next fall
and he wonders about teaching English.

Should I say to Joe
most kids today don't read Emerson
Thoreau Whitman Dickinson Crane Melville.
Some don't like Salinger.

But Joe reads Hawthorne Hemingway Fitzgerald
Manfred Rand Remarque Seattle Steinbeck.

At eighteen he's a retired defensive end
who's rediscovered the wonder of books.

Joe pointed out over the phone today
Salinger always includes children
as we discussed "For Esme With Love and Squalor."

I realized Joe's entered the adult world
and I wonder what I can tell him now?

(B)

A SMALL WINDOW

From a slow
gray press
of clouds

pages pile up
as they drop
piecemeal

to limestone blocks
ancient books
in freezing air.

Tapering black
trees curl into
quirky calligraphy.

On a quest to find
something lost
my wife

steps into our spare
room where I've
stopped writing.

Looking through a small
window she smiles
at the bald

head of an old
leather basketball
resting on a circle

of darker greener grass —
slowly growing back
its white hair.

(S)

STOP. SPEAK YOUR SONG

— to M.L. Hopson & Kathleen Hurley & Sam
who live their bliss

I didn't know, riding that Greyhound
through Utah on my way home from boot camp
in San Diego, or driving to interviews that first year
in Fort Dodge, Woodbine, Oelwein, Mason City,
Humboldt, North Scott — with offers from each.

Or five years later, advancing to Des Moines,
that I could STOP somewhere along the way
to communicate, to sing my story, tell my poem,
join an audience of expressive mindful people
who appreciate such a performance.

How didn't I hear it then? Shout it now?
Ring church bells like Emily Dickinson's father
in Amherst to proclaim a glorious sunrise,
call an assembly for poetry, music, drama,
dance, color, paint — another story or verse?

Itself. It's enough. Not just to please a boss,
C.O., or that actual racist superintendent
who began his "welcome back teachers" speech
with allusion to "a nigger in the woodpile . . ."
Disclaim. Turn away. Dance. Sing. Recite!

To hear the word, find your own ministry of call
to understand these voices, see those artists
who listen, pay attention, watch and respond.
Performers are invited. Marquart's Bone People.
Friends, family and colleagues smile and wait.

Your world is ready, more poet than historian.
So stop. Relax as much as you can.
Beat your drum. Sing your story. Paint
your drawing. Speak your song. Dance
your poem. Dream. And live your bliss.

(B)

VERMEER'S NAILS

He was faithful
even to a nail's
shadow, that small
slanting buoy around
which waves of light
flow from the left
of the milkmaid's
tilting head as she
looks down. Her
lavender and dark
yellow sleeves are
pushed up to her
powerful elbows
that pale in comparison
to her ruddy hands that also
helped the painter's family
outdoors by pinning
complicated freezing
17th century laundry
to icicle lines, and snapping
squawking chickens' stringy
necks, then plucking stinking
feathers in pails of hot water.
Her steady hands aim
milk's white braid
from a clay pitcher
into a clay bowl
with deft precision
just as Vermeer brushed
with precision the wicker
and brass baskets, the bread and light

filling our future eyes
through the shut window's
glass in Delft. Under
a navy blue apron
the girl's maroon skirt
looks solid as a column.
Even with eleven children
Vermeer patiently painted
the holes left by nails
pulled or fallen centuries ago
from the flaking wall's
reflected light.

(S)

Twenty Years After the Suicide

Mike are you listening
I can understand but
what I really need to know
is were there regrets

we found love bright
alive and striking
forever running
together with us

on tracks fields and courts
of our high school teams
but we graduated and
where was she for you Mike

we thought you had found her
as State Champion Coach
until you became Richard Cory
the athlete dying young

now what I want to know Mike
did you overplay the game
what I really need to know Mike
do you hear are you listening

(B)

Scratching A Sonnet In Huxley, Iowa (Circa 1968)

— for Paul Ragee (1946-1979)

Ostrich feathers are glued
to the purple brassiere of a lovely stripper
who dances until nude or gets booed.
I slip a pencil into the claw of my friend
strapped to a chair with wheels.
Sucking beer through a straw
he feels nothing
from his chest to his heels.
He strips a napkin from a silver box
and lays it by some salty peanuts, pretzels,
chips and other junk food on the table
where everyone talks. Pushing the pencil
with his locked hand, my paralyzed friend,
Paul, traps the napkin while scratching
a sonnet on it. He sends it to the bored
stripper who reads it, grinding her hips
to rock-and-roll on a jukebox.
She winks at Paul and slips his words
into her feathered brassiere
while he grins and sucks his straw.

The stripper is athletic like my friend,
a former pole-vaulter who dove
into shallow water in a quarry
snapping the nerves in his spine.
Feathers go flying when the stripper
flings her bra and drops her G-string
not much wider than a line of poetry
my friend scratched on the napkin
that also goes flying now the way my friend
flew when he pushed away his bent pole
and sailed over a balanced bar.

When the stripper's number is over
she grabs a robe and gathers her feathers,
G-string, bra and the napkin with my friend's
sonnet on it. He sucks his bubbling beer
through a straw, grins at her, rakes
another napkin from the silver box.

(S)

Good Croquet in the Sixties

— with thanks, for Don B.

You looked like Rock Hudson and you loved to suck
long cigars. You showed me how to play good croquet,
standing close behind me with your arms around me, your
hands guiding mine on the stiff mallet. You easily won
every game with your amazing aim and smooth follow through.

An actor, you also did stand-up in comedy clubs in Hollywood.
I read a crisp newspaper clipping announcing your appearance
on the Lassie TV show, with a yellowing photo of tall dark you
shaking Lassie #18's famous paw. Later you fixed spaghetti with
red wine and French bread for our first and last supper together.

That night you wrote Johnny Carson's best jokes in a black
three-ring binder and told some funny stories of your own.
You said I could share your only bed or flop on the floor.
I was tired of sleeping in boxcars, ditches and churches.
So I took your friendly offer. Barely into my first dream

your warm hand skimmed my young thigh. It felt great,
but I declined. You yawned and said, "Okay." Then we slept.
Next morning I watched you lick yellow eggs over easy
from the prongs of your fork. Your white-haired father
visited frowning. He picked up a package in your A-frame.

He looked like Alexander Calder eyeing me suspiciously
under big balanced white eyebrows. When he left, we swam
naked in a green quarry following your fifth victory
at croquet. We sunned our limbs like lizards on limestone
hunks scattered around the landscape like broken coffins.

You drove me to Boston so you could "shop for sailors."
Later, I met a guy at the Y who let me flop on his floor
for free. He flipped hamburgers in a greasy diner
and every night his penny loafers curled up at their
scuffed toes like used elf slippers. He was so lonely
he smuggled home sacks of hamburgers to bribe me to stay.

(S)

BUSINESS MODEL
ANT FARMS
IN CONSISTENT CLASSROOMS

The ant farm I was going to buy
for my boys and daughter
made me think of where I teach

in the open classrooms
with collapsible movable walls
in our open transparent society

and I wondered how long
the ants would survive
being shaken by the viewers
scrutinizing and appraising

with sociometric measures
within parameters of rigor and scope
and relevance of the role and intrinsic
values of our ant farm

and I decided not to buy it.

PRISONER OF SEX

Aren't we all ?

(B)

ABOUT THE POETS

Barry Benson has taught English and writing from 8th grade through community college, written news and feature stories for a weekly newspaper, and served as co-poetry editor (with Jody Speer) of a literary journal, *Stand Alone*. His poems are published in journals such as *Subtropics, North American Review, Plainsongs, Flyway, Spoon River Poetry Review, Terminus, Mid-American Poetry Review, Nassau Review, Comstock Review, Timber Creek Review, Brevities, The Iconoclast, Hidden Oak, Briar Cliff Review*, and others. He lives in Des Moines.

Steve Benson, a fourth generation Iowan, studied poetry with James Hearst at the University of Northern Iowa where he started out as a football-playing art major. He taught art in public schools, grades 1 through 12, for over 30 years. His poems have appeared in such literary journals as *The North American Review, MARGIE, Poet Lore, The Briar Cliff Review, Spoon River Poetry Review, Plainsongs, Quercus Review, The MacGuffin, Wisconsin Review*, and *The Hollins Critic*. Twenty of his poems have been published by *The Christian Science Monitor*. In 2003, seven of his poems were included in *The Dryland Fish: An Anthology of Contemporary Iowa Poets*. His chapbook, *A Light in the Kitchen*, was the winner of The 2001 Blue Light Poetry Prize. He lives with his wife and children in Mt. Vernon, Iowa.

No relation to me, but brothers in the guts of deep, dark, old, weird America, the viscera of heartland their shared family legends, firsthand feedback stirring one another's grief and energy along, resilient as cubs, memories crystals hard and sharp, these two linked different men are wrenchingly attentive to a restless, emphatic, and receptive, sensuous life in contact with and imagining the world they've known. Their poems' honest power braces against labor's compromises and intuition's leaps, tradition and discovery, to bring us into real places some of us have never been and others may not have left.

    —Steve Benson, Maine language poet (eight books published) and practicing psychologist (not related to Barry or Steve Benson).

Barry and Steve Benson for several years contributed poems to Plainsongs and it is a real pleasure to see a joint collection by the two brothers. Their styles are different, their subject matters often converge: their Iowa hard-scrabble childhood, the dense detail of working life, the broken relationships within family and marriage. Both men have turned to poetry for finding meaning in the dislocation and dissonance of experience. Barry's voice benefits from everything he has studied and read, from Francois Villon to Billy Collins — all mixed with his experiences in farm country, the navy, the English class room and literary editing. Barry's humor has something of Nathaniel West and Wright Morris: the peculiar and the grotesque — sort of the Faulkner effect in As I Lay Dying.

    Steve's poems focus on the wreckage of life's institutions, with poetry as the life preserver, the means of being with other people. Pared to their clearest language, his poems carry the cultural artifacts of the Iowan rural landscape. One poem (a Plainsongs award poem) brings a bar scene between father and son to life in detail.

    Both men are serious poets and I welcome their joint endeavor — a book that adds several layers of nuance and depth to the picture of bucolic Iowa life we received from The Music Man!

    —Dwight Marsh, Editor emeritus, Plainsongs

The Benson brothers, Barry and Steve, are the tag-team champions of poetry. In this unique co-authored masterpiece, the Bensons tour us through history and popular culture with school kids' enthusiasm and energy, romping through the waters of time like two heroes straight from the pages of Mark Twain. Savor and read slowly, there's a lot of ground to cover. But when you are finished you will have earned your Benson brothers' merit badge, qualifying you to spark fires straight from the imagination.

    —Rustin Larson, author of *Crazy Star* and *The Wine-Dark House*

Printed in the United States of America

LaVergne, TN USA
30 November 2009

165479LV00003B/226/P